HONEYMOON G

Written By:
Herbert I. Kavet

Illustrated By:
Martin Riskin

© 1992
by **Ivory Tower Publishing Company, Inc.**
All Rights Reserved

No portion of this book may be reproduced - mechanically, electronically, or by any other means including photocopying - without the permission of the publisher.

Manufactured in the United States of America

30 29 28 27 26 25 24 23 22 21 20 19 18 17 16 15 14 13 12 11 10 9 8 7 6 5 4 3

Ivory Tower Publishing Co., Inc.
125 Walnut Street
P.O. Box 9132
Watertown, MA 02272-9132
Telephone #: (617) 923-1111 Fax #: (617) 923-8839

HONEYMOON (hun´ē moon´)

Literally mooning with honey; from the stunt practiced by college kids of mooning passing traffic with honey on their asses.

HONEYMOONS ARE FRAUGHT WITH HIDDEN DANGERS, TO WIT:

There once was a couple named Kelly
who spent their lives belly to belly
Because, in their haste
They used library paste
Instead of petroleum jelly

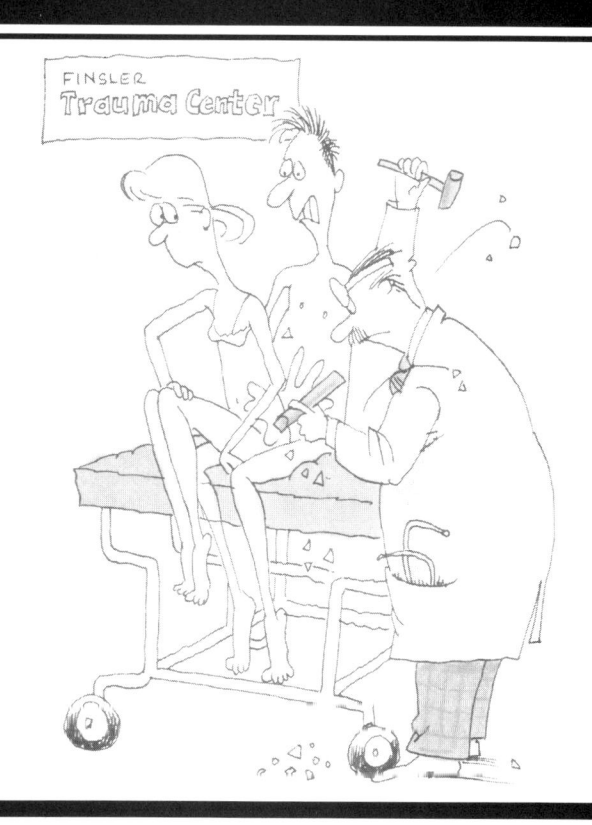

HONEYMOON FINANCES

Bride Pays For:

1. Vacuum service to get rice out of hair.
2. Whimsical underwear.
3. All calls home to mother.
4. Excess baggage costs for lubricants and bubble bath.
5. Vitamins and aphrodisiac tonics.

HONEYMOON FINANCES

Groom Pays for:

1. Speeding ticket on route to hotel.
2. Sex related damage to bed and walls.
3. All video tape equipment and rentals.
4. Sex toys whether kinky or capricious.
5. Tips to horrified chambermaid.

COMMON HONEYMOON ANXIETIES – GROOM

1. Getting rid of wedding guests.
2. How much to tip bellman?
3. Will bride snicker at your teddy bear?
4. Where can I find a G spot?

COMMON HONEYMOON ANXIETIES – BRIDE

1. Will he hurt me?
2. Will he not hurt me?
3. Will I have to fake orgasm for the entire week?
4. When should we dismiss the photographer?

WHAT WOMEN WANT MOST ON A HONEYMOON

Women want respect, lingering foreplay, love, sensitivity, consideration, affection, and lingering foreplay. Lingering afterplay is OK too.

WHAT MEN WANT MOST ON A HONEYMOON

Being allowed to sleep right afterwards without having to talk about love.

PICKING A HONEYMOON SPOT

Description

Whispering Pines

Secluded Beaches

Unspoiled Local Culture

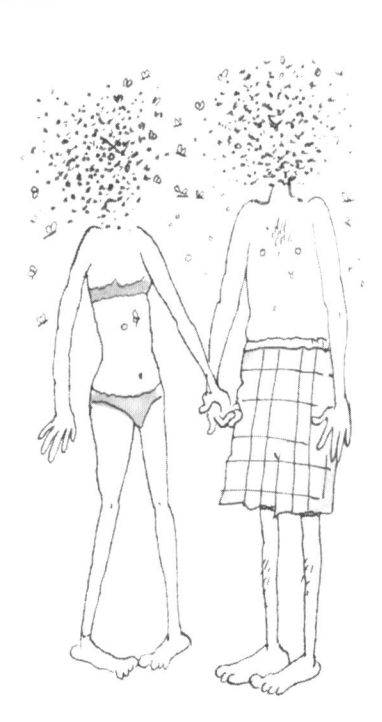

What they really mean

The mosquitos whisper all the way to your eardrum.

The locals never go there because of the alligators.

Murderous terrorism between the feuding ethnic groups.

PICKING A HONEYMOON SPOT

Description

Romantic Cruise

Bright Sunny Beaches

Cozy Cabins

What they really mean

Try not to throw up in the tiny cabin 'cause you'll never get rid of the smell.

The sunburn will prevent you from having sex the entire week.

You can't go outside because the bears will eat you.

WHO TO BRING ALONG ON YOUR HONEYMOON

This is strictly a personal decision based on what kind of honeymoon you want. With a housekeeping unit, Mom might be nice, especially if you are particularly partial to her brand of home cooking.

Tennis and golf partners are always a good choice especially if your game isn't quite compatible with your mate.

WHO TO BRING ALONG ON YOUR HONEYMOON

The inclusion of drinking buddies is generally in poor taste unless they know all the lyrics to "ai ai ai ai, In China they do it for chili."

Old boy or girl friends are permissible if you're not sure you'll have enough to talk to your hubby or wife about all week.

PACKING FOR THE HONEYMOON

Good Things to Bring on a Honeymoon

1. Your entire underwear collection
2. All your basic leather outfits
3. One Little-Bo-Peep costume
4. Bubble bath
5. Lubricating jelly
6. More lubricating jelly

PACKING FOR THE HONEYMOON

Bad Things to Bring:

1. Quart jars of ring cleanser
2. Phone numbers of old boyfriends or girlfriends
3. Flannel pajamas
4. Any sort of inflatable doll
5. Support pantyhose

MORE PACKING TIPS FOR THE HONEYMOON – GROOM

1. Vitamins are nice.
2. Don't load up on socks and underwear - it's OK to wash them in the sink.
3. Try to limit the sports equipment.
4. Your marriage will last longer if you always travel with separate suitcases.

MORE PACKING TIPS FOR THE HONEYMOON – BRIDE

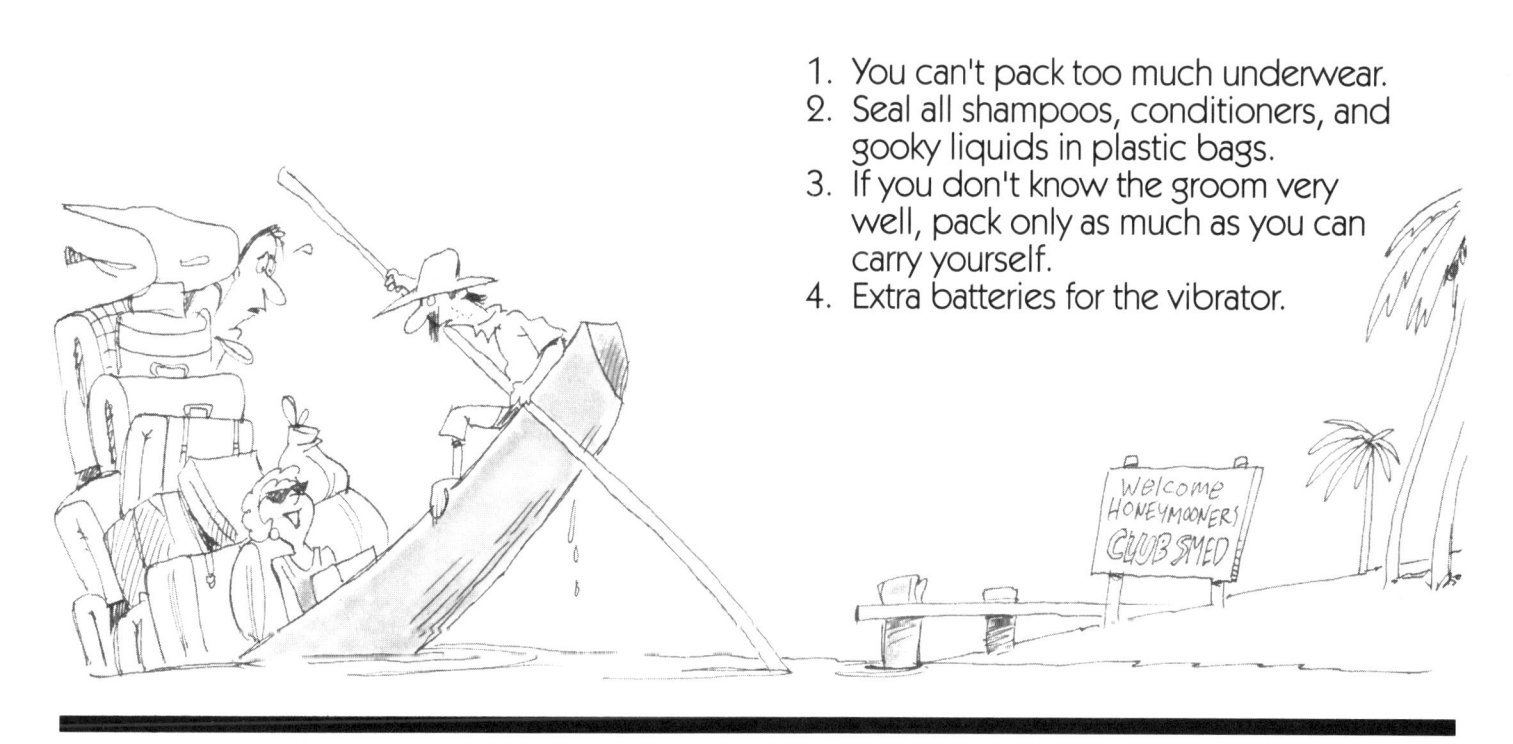

1. You can't pack too much underwear.
2. Seal all shampoos, conditioners, and gooky liquids in plastic bags.
3. If you don't know the groom very well, pack only as much as you can carry yourself.
4. Extra batteries for the vibrator.

REHEARSING THE WEDDING NIGHT

Traditional places to practice for the wedding night:

1. Back seat of your Toyota.
2. Your parents' living room couch.
3. Behind the gym.
4. In a motel room during the school's honors field trip.

REHEARSING THE WEDDING NIGHT

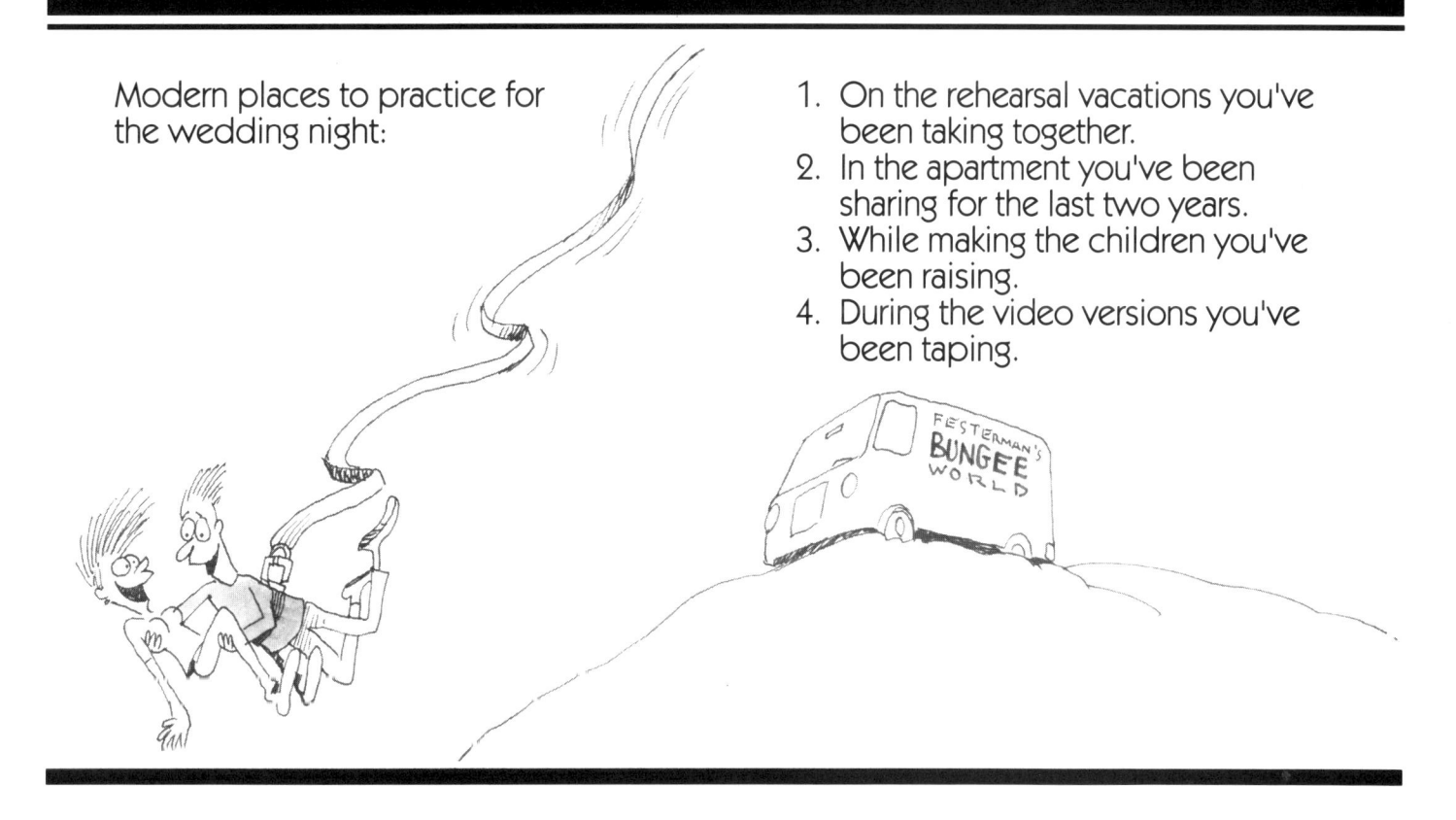

Modern places to practice for the wedding night:

1. On the rehearsal vacations you've been taking together.
2. In the apartment you've been sharing for the last two years.
3. While making the children you've been raising.
4. During the video versions you've been taping.

IN-FLIGHT LOVE MAKING

What is permissible under a blanket in an Air France first class seat can lead to imprisonment if you're on a five-across-coach-seat on British Airlines.

If you can't wait, choose your airline with care and please wait until they dim the lights.

IN-FLIGHT LOVE MAKING

Shy couples usually rely on the restrooms. You hear great stories but most of these toilets have trouble holding one normal size person. Two squirming lovers seems impossible. Besides, the floor is always wet. Actually, having sex in an airplane restroom is only asking for back troubles which will require Chiropractic visits for the rest of your life.

USING THE BATHROOM

Groom's Bathroom Activities:

1. Flexes muscles to assure manliness.
2. Brushes teeth and shaves chin if he remembers about whisker burns.
3. Scrutinizes and admires powerful loins.
4. Worries about farting under the covers.
5. Final words of encouragment to "Mr. Thunder Rod."

The bathroom is the final inviolable sanctuary remaining to you now that you're married.

USING THE BATHROOM

Bride's Bathroom Activities:

1. Examine face for last minute pimples.
2. Corrects posture to maximize appearance of bust.
3. Checks breath odor.
4. Applies scents to unadvertised places.
5. Ponders possible cellulite where thighs meet buttocks, if mirror permits.

SHARING THE BATHROOM ON YOUR HONEYMOON

This is the acid test of every honeymoon, indeed every marriage - How agreeably do you share the bathroom? It's all well and good to be in love with each other in the nuptial bed or all dressed up in gowns and tuxes but quite another when confronted in close proximity to each other's odors, emissions, and body hairs.

SHARING THE BATHROOM ON YOUR HONEYMOON

A wise couple will consider the following before vows are engaged:

Use of the bathroom as drying room
Position of toilet seat
Hair in the sink
Hair on the deodorant
Hairs anywhere

CAMPING ON YOUR HONEYMOON

DEALING WITH BUGS

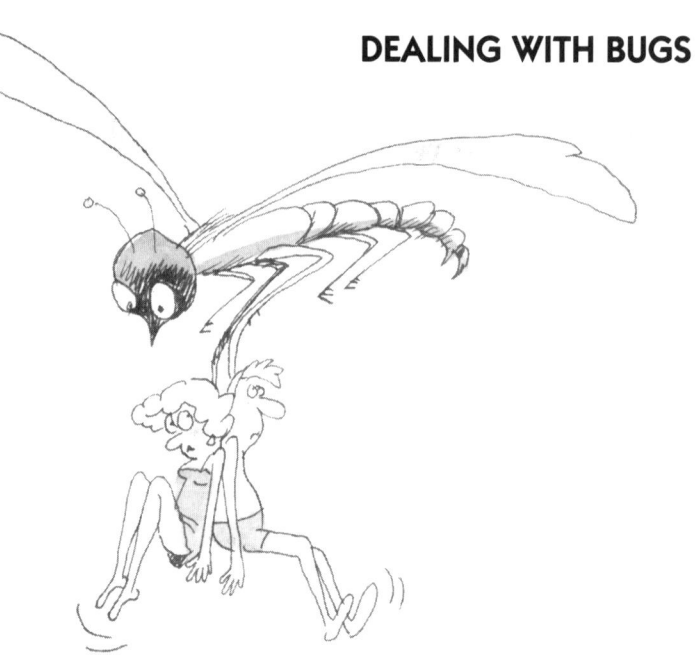

The easiest way to deal with mosquitoes, black flies, and other flying pests when you camp is to travel in the cooler months in which case you will freeze to death the whole time. Insect repellent works fine, of course, but constant use turns your skin white which when combined with the smell (the insect repellent and you) will also repel your spouse.

CAMPING ON YOUR HONEYMOON

PERSONAL HYGIENE

Hot showers and toilets certainly make cleanliness easier to achieve. Living in the woods for a week or two will introduce you to the real aroma and feel of your bodies, and if you can still make love under these circumstances, your marriage is truly made in heaven.

If it's warm enough to wash in lakes or streams, the bugs will probably eat you alive.

ADVANTAGES OF UNDRESSING IN THE DARK

1. It's easier to hide flab and embarrassing cellulite.
2. Avoids frightening an inexperienced bride.
3. Allows you to make all kinds of funny faces.
4. It gives you a chance to hide in case you decide you've made a terrible mistake.
5. Conceals any holes in your underwear.

ADVANTAGES OF UNDRESSING IN THE LIGHT

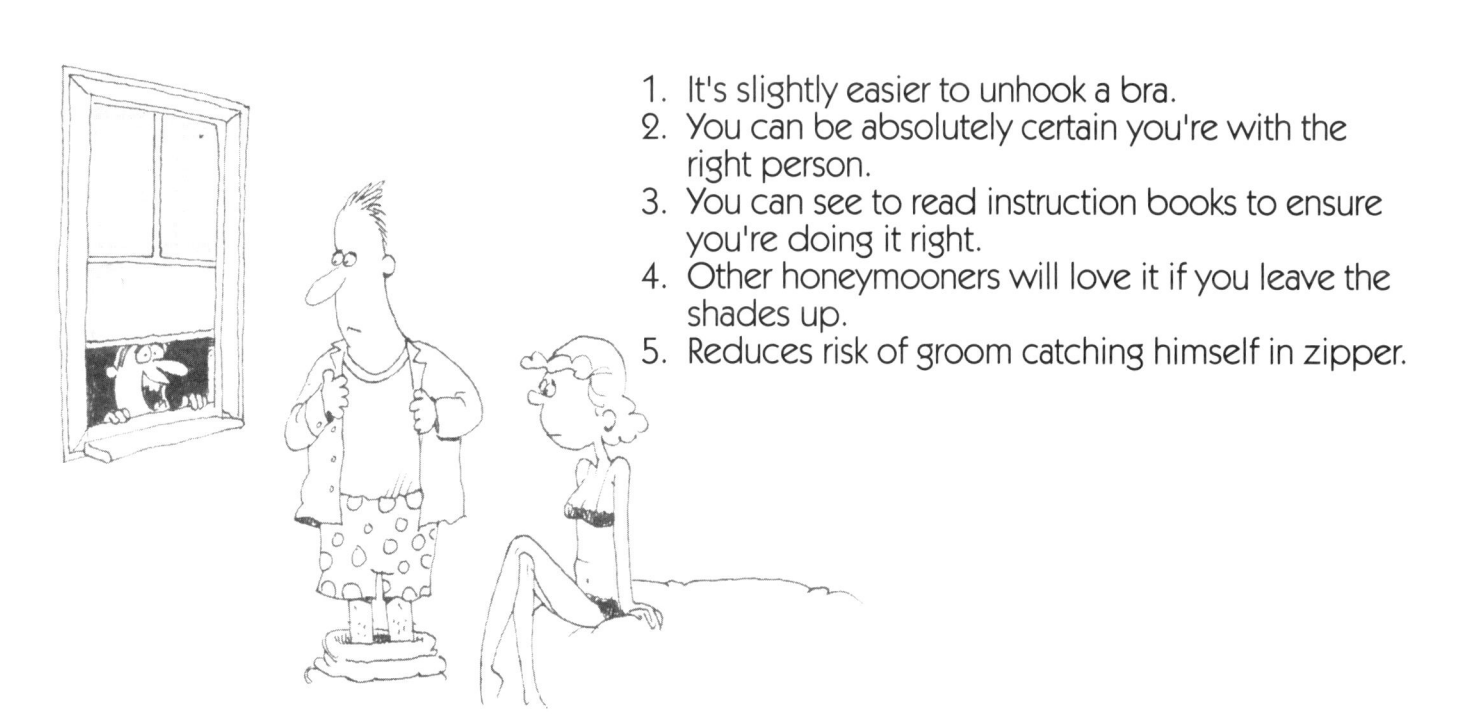

1. It's slightly easier to unhook a bra.
2. You can be absolutely certain you're with the right person.
3. You can see to read instruction books to ensure you're doing it right.
4. Other honeymooners will love it if you leave the shades up.
5. Reduces risk of groom catching himself in zipper.

WHAT GROOM DISCOVERS IF IT'S THE FIRST TIME

"Hey, this is like masturbating only you don't have to fantasize!"

WHAT BRIDE DISCOVERS IF IT'S THE FIRST TIME

"Hey, this is like playing with yourself only you don't climax."

VIRGINITY ON YOUR HONEYMOON

Virginity is a very nice thing to bring along on a honeymoon, as it adds to the anticipation and excitement. The groom, of course, has been bugging you to leave it at home, since before you were engaged. It doesn't matter much where you leave your virginity because men know practically nothing about it anyhow.

MEN AND VIRGINITY

1. 78% of men don't know what makes a virgin.
2. Of the remaining 22% only those who have been to medical school can spell HYMEN.
3. You can convince a sex crazed groom of anything.
4. If you tell him he's the biggest, best, smartest, or most amazing, he will forget all about virginity.
5. If the groom persists about your virginity, ask him to find your G spot and he will immediately roll over and feign sleep.

THE <u>GROOM</u> WILL KNOW THE MARRIAGE HAS BEEN CONSUMMATED IF

1. He takes more than 3 naps in the afternoon.
2. He skips the play-off games.
3. His "thunder-rod" takes on the consistency of overcooked linguini.
4. He doesn't care where his wife goes when she goes out as long as he doesn't have to go with her.
5. His wife doen't say UGH when he farts under the covers.

THE **BRIDE** WILL KNOW THE MARRIAGE HAS BEEN CONSUMMATED IF

1. She floats to the ceiling tingling with delight.
2. She awakes exhausted from a night of wild passion.
3. She achieves a simultaneous orgasm with her husband.
4. She no longer is embarrassed by sex toys.
5. She doesn't mind sharing his toothbrush.

SHOULD THE BRIDE FAKE ORGASM?

Do you know why so many brides fake orgasm?

It's because so many grooms fake foreplay.

BRIDES SHOULD FAKE ORGASM IF:

1. Groom is very insecure.
2. Groom is overly secure.
3. Groom is still in the bathroom.
4. Groom is delayed trying to untangle pantyhose from around ankles.

ETIQUETTE FOR GROOM

Try not to damage underthings during removal.
Try to look at bride's face while she's undressing.
Remember to put down toilet seat at night.
Ask politely, "Was it good for you too?"
Don't complain if forced to sleep on wet spot.
Tell bride you love her (4 times per hour).

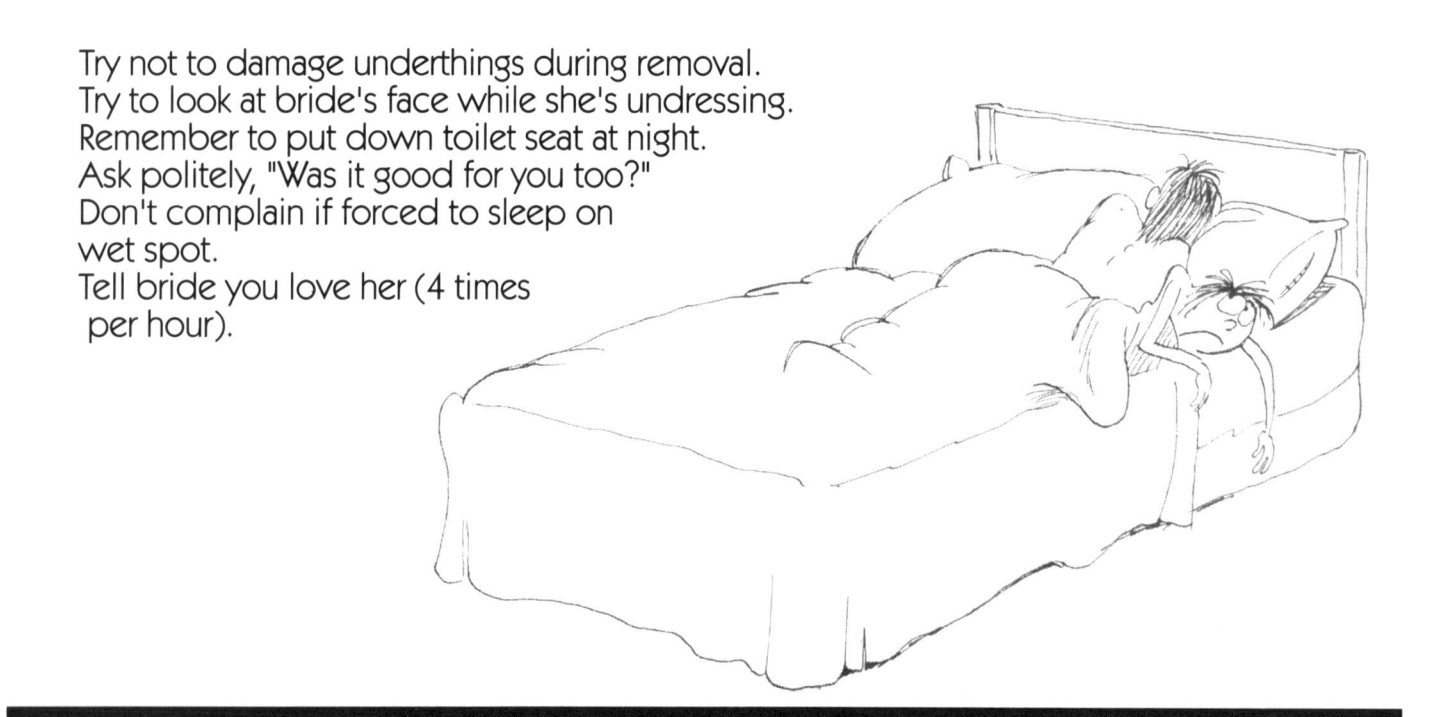

ETIQUETTE FOR BRIDE

Never show disappointment when groom undresses.
Ooooh and Aaaaah over all the groom's fumbling attempts.
Agree to do it to him if he does it to you.
Agree to cooperate in mild fantasies.
Wait until groom is asleep before phoning mother.

SOURCES OF SEXUAL PLEASURE – MALE

1. Talking dirty to guys in locker rooms
2. X-rated movies
3. Peeking down bodices
4. Viewing more than four square inches of female skin
5. Thinking about any of the above

SOURCES OF SEXUAL PLEASURE – FEMALE

1. No one really knows the source of female sexual pleasure

MULTIPLE ORGASMS ON YOUR HONEYMOON

Many people believe that each person is born with well, just so many orgasms for their whole life. Once you use them up, that's all you get. So lets say you're granted 1,682. It seems wasteful to use them up all at one sitting so to speak. Wouldn't it be more thrifty to space them out a little and then maybe they could last till you're 39 or 40?

MULTIPLE ORGASMS ON YOUR HONEYMOON

On the other hand, you wouldn't want to have any leftover orgasms when it's time for you to go to that great waterbed in the sky, and besides, what if this theory is wrong? There is hardly a more appropriate time to splurge than on your honeymoon.

Say, you don't suppose all those times in the bathroom with the dirty magazines count also?

HONEYMOON TURN-ONS

Heart shaped hot tubs
Eating pizza in the heart-shaped hot tub
Not having to lie to parents
Realizing your partner has tremendous imagination
Realizing your partner has tremendous endurance
Realizing your partner is tremendous

HONEYMOON TURN-OFFS

Frogs in the toilet
Really bad sun burns
Groom catching self in zipper in haste to undress
Sharing bath with a constipated Pakistani couple
A partner who keeps asking if you're done yet

GOOD THINGS TO SAY ON YOUR HONEYMOON

Oooooooh, it's so big.
I've never done this before.
No, no, my tongue never gets tired.
Can we do it again?
Oooooh, it's so tight.
Don't stop.

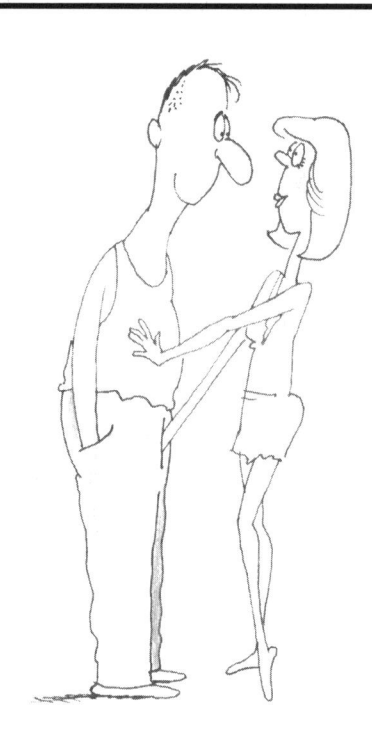

BAD THINGS TO SAY ON YOUR HONEYMOON

Is it in yet?
Have you ever done this with sheep?
You did it wrong.
Are you finished yet?
Don't think you can just go to sleep.
What did you say your name is?

MYSTERY OF THE GROOM

99.8% of all grooms can easily get an erection and 98% of all these erections are within 1/2 inch of all the others. I am not making this up. Why then do all these grooms think their particular erection will be a source of wonder and fascination to their brides? Everyone knows that only 2% of all brides are really amazed at their husband's erection and half of these are thrilled at what they see. The other half just think they forgot their contact lenses.

MYSTERY OF THE BRIDE

Why do all brides want to snuggle and talk of love afterwards instead of immediately rolling over and going to sleep?

HONEYMOON ACITIVITIES – THE NAP

If used as a euphemism for love making, a nap can be a lovely way to spend your honeymoon afternoons or mornings for that matter and to be honest, most honeymooners spend most of their time this way.

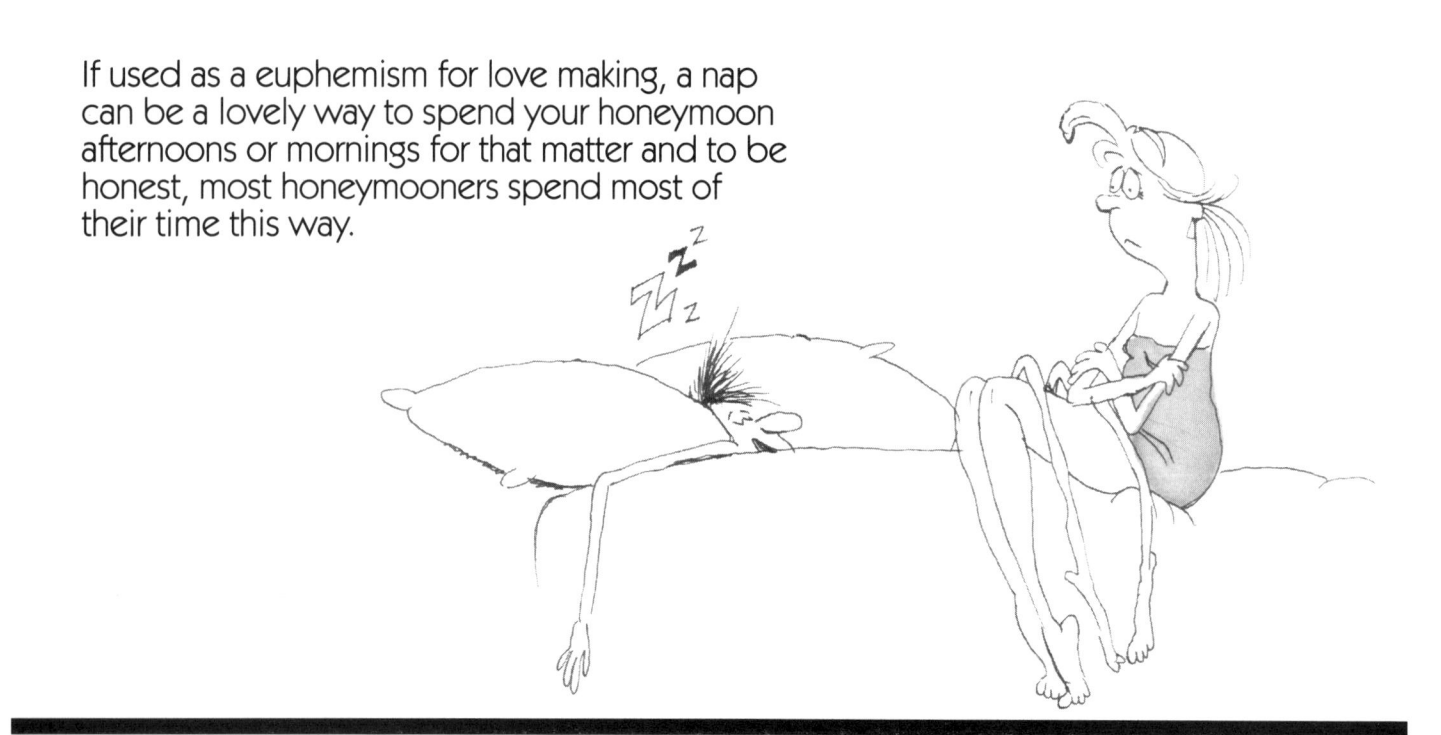

HONEYMOON ACTIVITIES – THE NAP

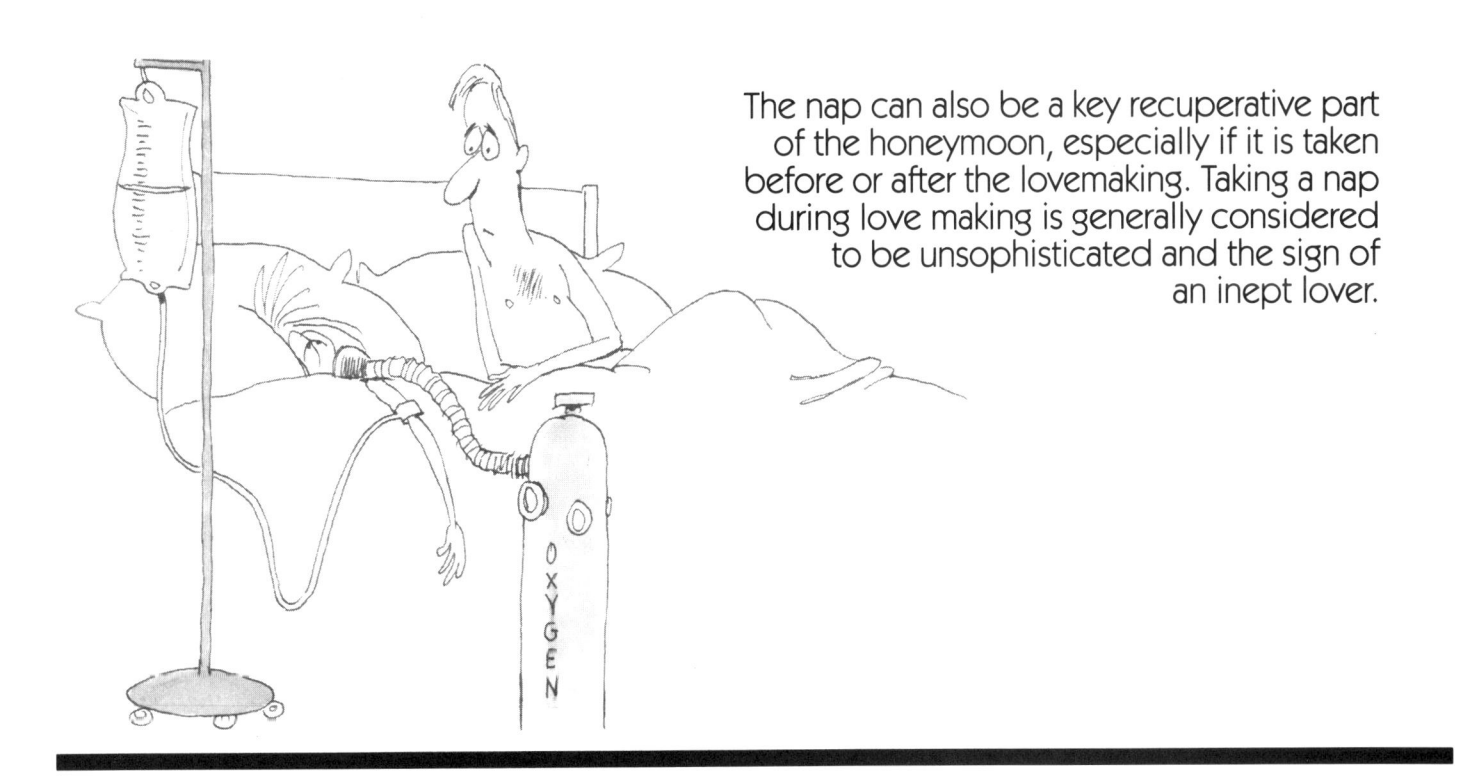

The nap can also be a key recuperative part of the honeymoon, especially if it is taken before or after the lovemaking. Taking a nap during love making is generally considered to be unsophisticated and the sign of an inept lover.

BUBBLES IN THE TUB

Champagne is real tickly - but expensive. Then again you can feel pretty tickly just drinking the stuff. Filling your mouth with the bubbly delight and then applying it to an erogenous zone (if you get my drift) works nicely if your honeymoon suite doesn't come with a tub that bubbles by itself.

BUBBLES IN THE TUB

A dab of bubble bath in the jacuzzi or whirlpool can add lots of fun to your bathtub games. It beats floating toy boats and duckies that's for sure. You can roll up your towels and jam them under the door to keep the foam from running out into the hall.

TYPICAL HONEYMOON ACITIVITIES

Backrubs

Sensuous, relaxing, healthful, revitalizing and of course backrubs usually lead to frontrubs.

Bouncing Up & Down in Bed

Many grooms think this is a perfectly adequate form of foreplay. Be careful not to lose your balance if you've chosen a water bed.

TYPICAL HONEYMOON ACTIVITIES

Call for Room Service

People think honeymooners can spend all week in bed with occasional breaks for nourishment provided by calls for room service. It makes a good story but most honeymooners have been living together for three years and would rather work on their tans at the beach.

Hunting for Bride's Contact Lens

If the groom is fortunate the search will take place around the sink and on the cold bathroom floor. More likely, you'll be performing this function in the sand on a moonlit beach with about a zero probability of success.

RAINY DAY HONEYMOON ACTIVITIES

Writing Thank-you Notes

This is a great honeymoon activity and these four sample letters should cover 99% of all your gifts.

Cash Gift:

Dear _____
Thank you very much for your generous gift. It came at a particularly appropriate time enabling my beloved to pay off those nasty parking tickets so we could get the car back for our honeymoon.

RAINY DAY HONEYMOON ACTIVITIES

Thank-you Notes

Can't Remember:

Dear _____

Thank you very much for whatever it was you gave us. We've probably grown very fond of it and knowing your generous nature, I'm sure we will find it a focal point of our life for many years to come.

RAINY DAY HONEYMOON ACITIVITIES

Thank You Notes

Your 12 juice blenders

Thank you very much for the lovely juice blender you gave us. It is much nicer than 7 of the others and somewhat more compact than 2, and a vastly better color than 3 that we received. We think we are going to use your juicer in the upstairs hall closet and hope you will be able to use it yourself when you come to visit.

Yours very truly,

RAINY DAY HONEYMOON ACTIVITIES

Thank You Notes

Your 200 bowls

Thank you very much for your lovely:
___ Salad   ___ Serving
___ Fruit   ___ Nut
___ Mixing

bowl. We are not exactly sure which one was yours but I'm sure it was one of the nice ones. We'll be filling it with peanuts or something when you come visit or maybe put it over your head for a haircut, ha ha.

Love,

GOOD WORDS TO USE IN POSTCARDS TO MOM

Loving
Romantic
Sensitive
Emotional

Treasure
Delight
Rapture
Poetic

GOOD WORDS TO USE IN POSTCARDS TO FRIENDS

Erotic
Enervating
Shameless
Profligate
Bestial

Ruttish
Dissolute
Lascivious
Bawdy
Carnal

STAYING IN YOUR ROOM

Years ago honeymooners used to stay in their room. This was before couples lived together for 2-3 years prior to getting married. Back in those days chambermaids still spoke English and knocked before walking into your room. They also put the chocolate mint on top of the pillow not underneath where it melts when you sleep.

STAYING IN YOUR ROOM

Nowadays of course, the chambermaids don't wait past 8:30 and barge in after a cursory knock that wouldn't give you time to zip your fly, and they will make up the room right around you without even noticing what you are doing.

LOSING WEIGHT ON YOUR HONEYMOON

Activity	Calories Burned
Romping on the beach	27 calories
Lovemaking on the beach	43 calories
If blanket got sandy	264 calories
Seeking medical aid to help sand problem	160 calories
Explaining sand problem to doctor	475 calories

LOSING WEIGHT ON YOUR HONEYMOON

Honeymoon Sex Fantasies

Activity	Calories Burned
Talking partner into fantasy	10-350 calories (depending)
Talking other honeymooners into your fantasy	190 calories
Getting them to do it right	25 calories
Organizing sex paraphernalia	18 calories
Explaining paraphernalia to customs agent	156 calories

LOSING WEIGHT ON YOUR HONEYMOON

Activity	Calories Burned
Carrying bride over transom	25 calories
Carrying groom over transom	38 calories
if groom has an erection	135 calories

Undressing

By self	20 calories
If mate is laughing at you	136 calories

LOSING WEIGHT ON YOUR HONEYMOON

Underthings

Activity	Calories Burned
Removing Panty hose	
By bride	8 calories
By groom	38 calories
If groom gets them tangled around ankles	165 calories
Forgetting to remove panty hose	575 calories
Removing Bra	
By bride	6 calories
By groom	36 calories
By groom with one hand	154 calories

HANDLING SICKNESS ON A HONEYMOON

72% of the thousands of honeymooners interviewed for this book report that they got sick enough on their honeymoon to want to call their mothers. That's carrying this "for better or worse" thing a little too far, I think. I mean who wants to clean up dinner remains for someone who is practically a stranger. If you believe these statistics, you'll borrow one of those little bags from behind the airline seats so your spouse can handle the problem by him or herself.

HANDLING SICKNESS ON A HONEYMOON

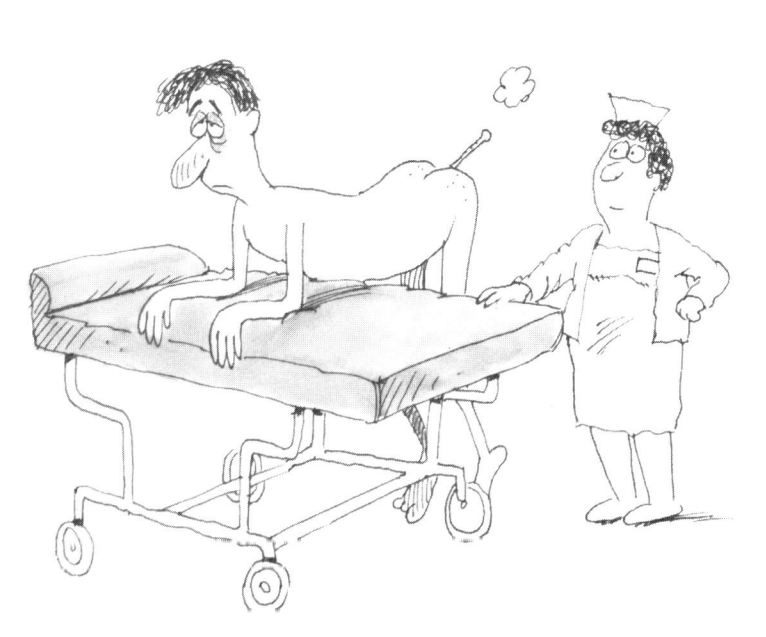

Usually only one partner gets sick on a honeymoon so you still have a 50-50 chance to have a good time. Just make sure your spouse is comfy and knows how to use the TV remote control and check out the pool for a few rays. If you're lonely, just team up with the healthy member of another honeymoon couple.

COMMON HONEYMOON PROBLEMS & SOLUTIONS

Problem	Solution
Toads in closet	Next time forget about the Amazon tour
Bride refuses to come out of bathroom	Introduce the leather outfit later in the week
Groom refuses to come out of bathroom	Switch immediately to bottled water

COMMON HONEYMOON PROBLEMS & SOLUTIONS

Problem

Bride screams "Gaaaarah" during orgasm

Partner's religious medallion keeps bashing you in the nose

Groom worn out

Solution

Teach her to quietly fake orgasm like all other women

It's time to get on top

Tie it to a Q-tip

PMS ON YOUR HONEYMOON

PMS ON YOUR HONEYMOON

I know, I know, the mother of the bride is supposed to plan and schedule the wedding so this doesn't happen. Tell that to the hormones that are dancing around your pituitary gland or whatever causes everything from salt craving to depression. Look, if you're faced with this problem, don't come to me. My wife has PMS 23 days out of the month.

WHAT TO DO IF THE BRIDE IS GAY

Look at the bright side. Your wife has found someone she can share clothes with, and you can probably learn a lot about sex by watching what they do to each other. Who knows, if you're lucky, you could get invited to join along.

WHAT TO DO IF THE GROOM IS GAY

This is one hell of a time to make this discovery and it certainly makes a case for a little premarital sex. Hell, maybe you'll like the guy he brings along better than your hubby.

MAKING IT LAST – GROOM

An inexperienced groom with a normal healthy libido can make it last for about 97 seconds including foreplay (if he knows what that is). An experienced groom, who knows his way around the farm, can go a little longer if it's the third time that night.

MAKING IT LAST – BRIDE

The average bride can make it last around 4 1/2 hours and can stay in an enraptured state of ecstasy the whole time and then will feel so exhilarated that she will want to stay up two more hours talking about it.

HONEYMOONING IN FOREIGN COUNTRIES

The biggest problem honeymooning overseas is getting used to the funny toilets and weird toilet paper. That's if you're lucky. Some people honeymoon where the toilet is only a hole in the floor with a strap to hold on to and no Westerners know quite what to do with that. An adventurous honeymoon in the Middle East involves figuring out how to use the little tin can of water that substitutes for toilet paper in what passes for a toilet. Good luck.

HONEYMOONING IN FOREIGN COUNTRIES

"OH NO, WE HAD TO EXPERIENCE THE REAL MEXICO."

HONEYMOONING IN FOREIGN COUNTRIES

One great advantage of honeymooning in foreign countries is that you'll make hard and fast friends with whatever other Americans, Canadians, Britishers, or other people speaking approximate English, that you meet. Nothing brings countrymen together faster than a horde of natives trying to sell you a rug or blanket.

HONEYMOONING IN FOREIGN COUNTRIES

Getting Your Sex Aids Through Customs

Don't grin. Don't look guilty. Just stand there with a straight face and insist they are therapeutic devices for your wife's bad neck.

VIDEO TAPING YOUR HONEYMOON

Good things to videotape:

1. Golden beaches that stretch to the sunset
2. Quaint cobblestone villages
3. Lush forests sprinkled with sparkling pools
4. Scintillating night life shows
5. The next door honeymoon couple who do it on the terrace.

VIDEO TAPING YOUR HONEYMOON

Inappropriate things to videotape:

1. Screwing your brains out
2. Bride's battle with control-top pantyhose
3. Groom's inability to do "it" again
4. Bride and Groom throwing up after 16 margaritas on the moonlight booze cruise.

HONEYMOON SEX RECORDS

The brilliantly innovative groom on top - bride underneath position was invented by Richard and Marybeth Schollhonser in 1957. They were able to sustain this position for an amazing 3 hours 22 minutes. Marybeth retained her virginity the entire time.

MOST IMAGINATIVE LOVEMAKING POSITIONS

HONEYMOON SEX RECORDS

MOST INEPT LOVER

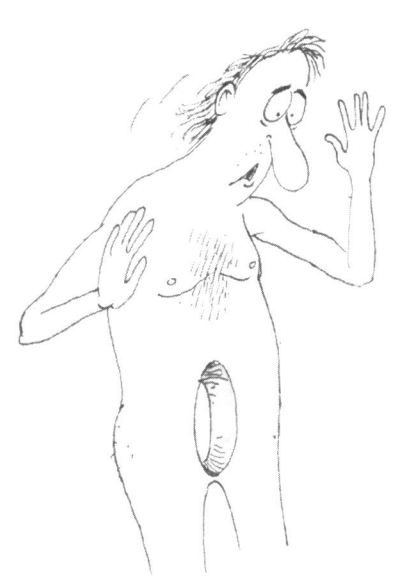

Harris and Penny Wuglethrope started on their wedding night and continued for 16 months. All the time Penny was saying "It's all right dear, I understand. It's nothing to worry about, we can be perfectly happy." Once she finally shut up, Harris got it up in about 13 seconds.

HONEYMOON SEX RECORDS

Purcy Hingglesworth and his bride Mildred were so worrried about safe sex that they took separate honeymoons. Mildred went to the Poconos where she spent the entire week scrubbing the heart-shaped bath tub. Purcy visited Niagra Falls and lost his virginity clutching the rail on the Maid Of The Mist Boat.

MOST CONCERNED ABOUT SAFE SEX

HONEYMOON SEX RECORDS

SMALLEST TIP TO BELLMAN

Chester Pierce handed the bellman at the Greenacres Hotel in Orlando a 7¢ tip after his bride, Glenda reminded him of this obligation. The disappointed and bewildered bellman hung around the nuptual room the entire night with his hand out.

HONEYMOON SEX RECORDS

In 1973, Paul and Dana Guggliano spent an entire week in their honeymoon suite at the Palace Hotel in Fez Morracco. Paul had the worst stomach upset ever treated in North Africa and Dana was too sunburned to put on clothes.

LONGEST TIME IN HONEYMOON SUITE

HONEYMOON SEX RECORDS

SUPERIOR ACCOMPLISHMENT OF LOVEMAKING

Tricia and Morton Leary achieved a simultaneous orgasm on the first night of their honeymoon. They had been living together for 7 years and this was the 2463rd time they had sex. Later Morton said, "I always knew it would happen if she'd just relax."

SIGNS OF HONEYMOON FATIGUE – GROOM

1. Would rather watch TV
2. Stops staring at topless bathers
3. Uncontrollable urge for jelly donuts
4. Urinates, sitting down

SIGNS OF HONEYMOON FATIGUE – BRIDE

1. Starts calling sorority sisters
2. Constantly craves chocolate
3. Incontinent in mornings
4. Regrets not bringing flannel pajamas

RATING YOUR HONEYMOON

Your lovemaking is totally compatible if neither party asked how the other is doing, someone volunteers a kiss before falling asleep, you share the blankets nicely and neither bride nor groom are terribly disturbed by loud farting.

RATING YOUR HONEYMOON

Your lovemaking is only partially compatible if one partner has cold feet and/or sharp toe nails, you can't stand the thought of kissing before brushing your teeth in the morning and your mate moves only to go to the bathroom.

CONSUMMATING YOUR MARRIAGE

Intercourse is a fine way to consummate your marriage, but other perfectly legal methods also may be used.

1. Showering together with lights off
2. Sharing a teddy bear for two nights in a row
3. Becoming aroused by some X-rated videos
4. French kissing in the morning before brushing teeth
5. Using the same deodorant stick

HOW TO TELL WHEN THE HONEYMOON IS OVER

The honeymoon is over when

I DO
becomes
I WON'T.

Other books we publish are available at many fine stores. If you can't find them, send directly to us. $7.00 postpaid

2400-How To Have Sex On Your Birthday. Finding a partner, special birthday sex positions, kinky sex on your birthday and much more.

2402-Confessions From The Bathroom. There are things in this book that happen to all of us that none of us ever talk about. The Gas Station Dump, for example, or the Corn Niblet Dump, the Porta Pottie Dump and more.

2403-The Good Bonking Guide. Bonking is a great new British term for doing "you know what". Covers bonking in the dark, bonking all night long, improving your bonking, and everything else you've ever wanted to know.

2407-40 Happens. When being out of prune juice ruins your whole day and you realize anyone with the energy to do it on a weeknight must be a sex maniac.

2408-30 Happens. When you take out a lifetime membership at your health club, and you still wonder when the baby fat will finally disappear.

2409-50 Happens. When you remember when "made in Japan" meant something that didn't work, and you can't remember what you went to the top of the stairs for.

2411-The Geriatric Sex Guide. It's not his mind that needs expanding; and you're in the mood now, but by the time you're naked, you won't be!

2412-Golf Shots. What excuses to use to play through first, ways to distract your opponent, and when and where a true golfer is willing to play.

2414-60 Happens. When your kids start to look middle-aged, when software is some kind of comfortable underwear, and when your hearing is perfect if everyone would just stop mumbling.

2416-The Absolutely Worst Fart Book. The First Date Fart, The Oh My God Don't Let Me Fart Now Fart, The Lovers' Fart, The Doctor's Exam Room Fart and many more.

2417-Women Over 30 Are Better Because... Their nightmares about exams are starting to fade and their handbags can sustain life for about a week with no outside support whatsoever.

2418-9 Months In The Sac. A humorous look at pregnancy through the eyes of the baby, such as: why do pregnant women have to go to the bathroom as soon as they get to the store, and why does baby start doing aerobics when it's time to sleep?

2419-Cucumbers Are Better Than Men Because... Cucumbers are always ready when you are and cucumbers will never hear "yes, yes" when you're saying "NO, NO."

2421-Honeymoon Guide. Every IMPORTANT thing to know about the honeymoon — from The Advantages Of Undressing With The Light On (it's slightly easier to undo a bra) to What Men Want Most (being allowed to sleep right afterwards without having to talk about love).

2422-Eat Yourself Healthy. Calories only add up if the food is consumed at a table. Snacking and stand up nibbling don't count. Green M&M's are full of the same vitamins found in broccoli and lots of other useful eating information your mother never told you.

2423-Is There Sex After 40? Your wife liked you better when the bulge above your waist used to be the bulge in your trousers. You think wife-swapping means getting someone else to cook for you.

2424-Is There Sex After 50? Going to bed early just means a chance to catch up on your reading or watch a little extra t.v., and you find that you actually miss trying to make love quietly so as not to wake the children.

2425-Women Over 40 Are Better Because... Over 90 reasons why women over 40 really are better: They realize that no matter how many sit-ups and leg raises they do, they cannot recapture their 17-year-old figures—but they can find something attractive in any 21-year-old guy.

2426-Women Over 50 Are Better Because... More reasons why women over 50 are better: They will be amused if you take them parking, and they know that being alone is better than being with someone they don't like.

2427-You Know You're Over The Hill When... You tend to repeat yourself. All the stories of your youth have already bored most acquaintances several times over. Even worse, you've resigned to being slightly overweight after trying every diet that has come along in the last 15 years.

2428-Beer Is Better Than Women Because (Part II)... A beer doesn't get upset if you call it by the wrong name; and after several beers, you can roll over and go to sleep without having to talk about love.

2429-Married To A Computer. You're married to a computer if you fondle it daily, you keep in touch when you're travelling and you stare at it a lot without understanding it. You even eat most meals with it. Truly advanced computers are indistinguishable from coke machines.

2430-Is There Sex After 30? By the time you're 30, parking isn't as much fun as it was in high school. He thinks foreplay means parading around nude in front of the mirror, holding his stomach in; and she has found that the quickest way to get rid of an unwanted date is to start talking about commitment.

2431-Happy Birthday You Old Fart! You're an Old Fart when you spend less and less time between visits to a toilet, your back goes out more than you do, you tend to refer to anyone under 40 as a "kid," and you leave programming the VCR to people under 25.

2432-Big Weenies. Why some people have big weenies while other people have teenie weenies; how to find big weenies in a strange town; rating a weenie; as well as the kinds of men who possess a putz, a prong, a schwanz, a member, a rod and a wang—and more!

2433-Games You Can Play With Your Pussy. Why everyone should have a pussy; how to give a pussy a bath (grease the sides of the tub so it won't be able to claw its way out); dealing with pussy hairs (shellac it so the hairs stay right where they belong); and everything else you ever wanted to know about pussies.

2434-Sex And Marriage. What wives want out of marriage (romance, respect and a Bloomingdale's Charge Card); what husbands want out of marriage (to be left alone when watching football games and to be allowed to go to sleep after sex).

Ivory Tower Publishing Co., Inc., 125 Walnut St., P.O. Box 9132, Watertown, MA 02272-9132   Tel: (617) 923-1111